# ALIA'S MISSION

## SAVING THE BOOKS OF IRAQ

### Inspired by a True Story

## Mark Alan Stamaty

Alfred A. Knopf

NEW YORK

For Janet Schulman

THIS IS A BORZOI BOOK PUBLISHED BY ALFRED A. KNOPF

Copyright © 2004 by Mark Alan Stamaty

All rights reserved under International and Pan-American Copyright Conventions. Published in the United States by Alfred A. Knopf,
an imprint of Random House Children's Books, a division of Random House, Inc., New York, and simultaneously in Canada by Random House of Canada Limited,
Toronto. Distributed by Random House, Inc., New York.

KNOPF, BORZOI BOOKS, and the colophon are registered trademarks of Random House, Inc.

www.randomhouse.com/kids

*Library of Congress Cataloging-in-Publication Data*
Stamaty, Mark Alan.
Alia's mission : saving the books of Iraq / by Mark Alan Stamaty. — 1st ed.
p.   cm.
ISBN 0-375-83217-3 (trade) — ISBN 0-375-93217-8 (lib. bdg.)
1. Baker, Alia Muhammad—Juvenile literature. 2. Librarians—Iraq—Basrah—Biography—Juvenile literature.
3. Libraries—Iraq—Basrah—Juvenile literature. 4. Iraq War, 2003—Destruction and pillage—Juvenile literature. I. Title.
Z720.B24S73 2004
020'.92—dc22
2004048633

Printed in the United States of America
December 2004
10 9 8 7 6 5 4 3 2 1
First Edition

EVERY MORNING, ALIA DRIVES TO WORK. OFTEN, SHE WORRIES ABOUT THE PROBLEMS OF THE WORLD, BUT DEEP IN HER HEART IS A FEELING OF JOY.

ALIA LOVES HER JOB...

...AS CHIEF LIBRARIAN OF BASRA CENTRAL LIBRARY...

...SURROUNDED BY HER FAVORITE THINGS OF ALL: BOOKS!

EVER SINCE ALIA WAS A LITTLE GIRL, BOOKS HAVE BEEN A SOURCE OF HAPPINESS AND ADVENTURE FOR HER.

BOOKS HAVE TAUGHT HER ABOUT MANY THINGS, LIKE THE LONG AND FASCINATING HISTORY OF THE VERY LAND SHE LIVES ON...

...OF MANY TRIBES AND CIVILIZATIONS, OF KINGS AND CONQUERORS SINCE ANCIENT TIMES.

FROM BOOKS, ALIA HAS LEARNED ABOUT THE RISE OF THE GREAT MUSLIM CIVILIZATION 1,300 YEARS AGO, WHICH BUILT ASTONISHING CITIES AND LED THE WHOLE WORLD IN TRADE, SCIENCE, AND CULTURE.

AND BOOKS HAVE TAUGHT HER, TOO, OF THE FRIGHTFUL MONGOL INVASION 500 YEARS LATER, WHICH ENDED THAT CELEBRATED ERA AND BROUGHT THE DESTRUCTION BY FIRE OF THE GREAT BAGHDAD LIBRARY AND THE LOSS OF ITS IRREPLACEABLE TREASURES.

ALL DAY LONG, ALIA THINKS ABOUT WHAT TO DO. BY LATE AFTERNOON, SHE HAS AN IDEA.

AT QUITTING TIME, ALIA GOES TO A SHELF IN A BACK CORNER AND FILLS HER HANDBAG WITH BOOKS. THEN SHE HIDES TWO MORE ARMFULS UNDER HER SHAWL.

BEARING THE BULKY LOAD, SHE WALKS AS NORMALLY AS POSSIBLE PAST THE GOVERNMENT WORKERS, DOWN THE HALLWAY, THROUGH THE LOBBY, AND OUT OF THE LIBRARY.

BY THE TIME SHE REACHES HER CAR, HER ARMS AND SHOULDERS ARE ACHING KNOTS, HER HANDS NUMB AND TINGLY.

SHE LOOKS ALL AROUND HER TO MAKE SURE NO ONE IS WATCHING, THEN LOADS THE BOOKS INTO THE TRUNK AND GOES BACK FOR MORE.

THE GOVERNMENT WORKERS— PREOCCUPIED WITH THE WAR—TAKE LITTLE NOTICE OF THE COMINGS AND GOINGS OF A FEMALE LIBRARIAN.

IN SEVERAL TRIPS, ALIA MANAGES TO FILL THE TRUNK AND BACKSEAT, COVERING THE BOOKS CAREFULLY WITH A RUG AND A SHAWL. THEN SHE DRIVES HOME.

HER HUSBAND HELPS HER CARRY THE BOOKS INTO THEIR HOUSE. THEY STACK THEM NEATLY IN THE CLOSET.

A SHORT WHILE LATER, THEY SWING INTO ACTION.

ONE GROUP REMOVES BOOKS FROM THE SHELVES AND STACKS THEM CAREFULLY BY THE BACK DOOR OF THE LIBRARY.

A SECOND GROUP CARRIES THEM OUTSIDE TO A HIGH WALL THAT SEPARATES THE LIBRARY PROPERTY FROM ANIS'S RESTAURANT.

THE BOOKS ARE HANDED OVER THE WALL TO A THIRD GROUP, WHICH CARRIES THEM INTO THE RESTAURANT, PLACING THEM IN TALL STACKS.

IT IS A VERY BIG JOB. THEY WORK ALL DAY AND ALL NIGHT. IN THE LIGHT OF DAWN, THEY ARE STILL WORKING. EVERYONE IS TIRED, BUT THEY STAY AT IT, SPURRED ON BY DISTANT SOUNDS OF WAR.

**Alia's story is just the latest chapter in a long and fascinating history of libraries in Iraq and the Middle East. Here are some other stories you might not know....**

• The land now called Iraq was actually the birthplace of all written language. Over five thousand years ago, in approximately 3500 BCE, the ancient Sumerians used split reeds from local marshes to make wedge-shaped markings on tablets of wet clay. When baked in the hot sun, the clay held permanent impressions; we now call these writings "cuneiform." Collections of these cuneiform tablets made up the world's first-ever libraries.

• The ancient Middle Eastern city of Ebla, in present-day Syria, had an extensive palace library, with over fifteen thousand clay tablets stored on wooden shelves. The entire city was destroyed by Akkadian invaders in 2250 BCE, but in 1980 an Italian archaeologist stumbled upon over two thousand of the clay documents still intact!

How did these tablets survive over *four thousand years* of nature's wear and tear? After all, of over 500,000 texts held in the great Alexandrian Library of Egypt—built almost two thousand years after Ebla was destroyed—absolutely *nothing* remains. Both libraries were burned to the ground; what made such a difference at Ebla?

The difference was that the manuscripts in Alexandria's library were papyrus—thin paper-like scrolls made from stripped, pressed plant stalks. Much like paper, papyrus burns very easily; the blaze that destroyed the Alexandrian Library in the late 200s CE turned its collection to ash. With Ebla's clay tablets, though, fire only baked them harder, making them even more durable. By burning Ebla down, its conquerors unknowingly *protected* the city's literature!

• The story of the burning of the great Baghdad library, the Nizamiyah, which made such an impression on Alia as a child, occurred during the Mongol invasion of 1258 CE. In only one week, Mongol leader Hulagu Khan ravaged almost all of the city's thirty-six public libraries. Legend has it that so many books were thrown into the Tigris River that the water ran blue from their ink.

• The Nizamiyah library was severely damaged but not destroyed by the Mongol invasions. In fact, it still stands today, the third-oldest library in the world. Alia's library, too, has survived hardships. Extensive repairs to the Basra Central Library are currently in progress. The library will undergo a complete refurbishment, paving the way for new services such as a computer lab with Internet access and a summer-school program for local children. Most importantly, though, the library will continue to house the tens of thousands of books Alia and her friends worked so hard to protect, the precious cultural history of Iraq.

To learn how you can help preserve libraries, please contact the International Relations Department of the American Library Association at 1-800-545-2433.